BEHIND THE BLUE

BEHIND THE BLUE

Poetry & Prose

SHARON ARSEGO

Swirl Ink Publications

Contents

For my sister unit, Natalie

You are our family's sanctuary
and we are grateful for it, for you
always

You are the homestead that welcomes us
when we are most weary
where celebrations mean
lovingly prepared foods
and where your pride
and pleasure
in sustaining us
is palpable

From the Author

DEAR READER,

In the final weeks of writing and publishing *Behind the Blue,* I was met with a sobering diagnosis: Grade 1 Stage 1A Uterine Cancer. This revelation followed six months of symptoms, delays and hurdles outside of my control, and then, finally, wonderful doctors who would prove to be my champions. There were also two surgeries in twelve days. To say it was a lot to process at once is an understatement.

As I write this, I'm recovering from the second surgery, the one that saved my life. Yes, that's right, it saved my life. The surgery to remove the cancer did in fact cull all of it from my body. This is a wonderful, humbling result. There will, of course, be regular screenings in place for the next five years, and I'm committed to doing all I can to keep the disease from returning.

Now, with our family's health history, the blessing of a quick and satisfying outcome is not lost on me. I do cry spontaneous tears of relief and joy. My heart is equal parts grateful and proud. Grateful for people like my sister unit who was my number one ally throughout this process and pleased with myself for meeting this head on at the first sign of trouble. I can't emphasize enough the importance of advocating for yourself and your loved ones when facing health concerns. It can be exhausting, but it's necessary.

I say all this for two reasons: one is to raise awareness of Uterine Cancer and the importance of early detection, and the other is to provide some background on this new collection.

Prior to my health issue, *Behind the Blue* was already themed with movement from darkness into light, from sadness to hope. It was already emotional for me with poems like "Heartbroken" and "Now I Lay Me Down to Sleep". It all took on renewed meaning for me though in the days that followed me hearing the words, "You have cancer."

Those words lifted the fog I didn't know was hanging over me. In an instant, everything came into focus, crystallizing this poetry collection for me. It was a moment that struck deeply while also steadying me when I needed it most. Life sure does have a way, doesn't it?

Thank you for choosing to spend time with me between these pages. Should you find yourself facing a difficult time or situation, either now or in the future, it's my hope that reading some, or all of *Behind the Blue* speaks to you in an especially meaningful way.

Living in Hope,
Sharon

BEHIND THE BLUE

Poetry & Prose

SHARON ARSEGO

Prologue

An old soul still searching

The Maiden, the Mother, and the Crone

The full indigo moon lounges elegantly in a muted gray sky
Muted gray as cobalt creases form in the recesses of her mind
Her mind in shades of azure against the morning light
Light that reflects in her ancient, sapphire eyes
Eyes that her handmaidens
bathe with their tears
Tears shimmering,
remembering,
reflecting inward
Inward towards an old soul
An old soul still searching
Searching, intently seeking,
hopefully finding
Finding with capable hands that know how to carry burdens
Burdens, babies, worries, endearments, loves and losses
Losses gained while reaching to embrace
Embracing an engulfing massive stillness
A stillness that is the whole of the Universe
The whole of a Universe, from pinprick precision to infinity
Infinity upon infinity, defining the depth of her memory
Memories marred by an aquamarine mood
The mood of a burgeoning, tired heart
A tired heart infused with gaping grief
Grief dancing with a swelling sadness
A sadness gently lifted by the fullest of indigo moons
lounging elegantly in a muted gray sky

Nightshade

In the night there are shadows of shadows

In the night there are shadows of shadows
They grow deeper, darker than at day's beginning, or its end
It's in the night when our fears, our worries, settle
ferment, become more concentrated into their darkest
purest, most acidic and toxic forms

Their cheerless nature remains thoroughly unmoved
even when in the presence of beauty
or when surrounded by happy, though momentary, distractions

It's at night when our demons remove their masks
revealing our worst nightmares come to life
Uninhibited, these monsters dance with disdain before us
they taunt us, sneer at us, go nose to nose with us
With their rancid breath smelling of death
their cold, bony fingers, and their predatory gazes
they size us up for a slow kill

Chills combine with fear in an attempt to push us off the edge

It's at night when our demons remove their masks
to dance with disdain before us while we
we creatures of the dawn, the day, even the dusk
we weep for the lack of light

Sleep is not enough
I want to be unconscious
Feel
see
know nothing

from Cadence: Poems - April 2023

Digging deep
wanting a sense that all will be well

Digging deep
sifting through the sand and silt
looking for the lost keys to safeguard my sanity

If God is waiting for me to hit rock bottom, please tell him I just passed the last bit of the ledge and I'm on my way down.

The End

I passed by the bedroom stopping at the door
and in your face I read chapters I'd never seen before
A story I didn't recognize, one I didn't understand
yet in that moment I knew, our end was close at hand

Heartbroken

I love you, of that there is no doubt
and of course, I love myself, too
but my heart is big enough to fully hold us both
to be brave enough for the challenges ahead
to champion life together in the face of the world

A lifetime isn't enough, as lovers are prone to say
We have right now, we have this moment
and this one, and this one added to the next
It can add up to forever if that's what we desire

Let's remember this when life gets ugly
unkind, hard to talk about
Let's remember we have this moment
and this one, and this one added to the next
and to the next, adding up to forever

We have this time, here and now
Let's not waste it
not shut down or shut each other out

This is what I said to you under a summer sky peppered with stars
while we sat, parked in our first car, where the stones met the sand
where we watched the sun set, which was so cliche and yet so sweet
It was then, of your own choosing, you vowed to forsake the sea
and with both eyes open, I believed you

Now, a few years later, you sit facing away from me
My own face forced in the direction of your mounting betrayals
I'm left to grapple with too many dark truths

in this moment
and this one
and this one added to the next
and to the next
and to the next
Every one of them adding up to forever

We won't grow old together, as you often quipped
as we fell together in the middle of our lives
into the middle of our bed, while holding hands

Instead, I will remain alone with this moment
and this one
and this one added to the next
and to the next
and to the next
all of them adding up to my new forever

Forever heartbroken
in this moment
and this one
and this one added to the next
and to the next
and to the next

Broken Me inside
No matter the work I do
always need more glue

from Cadence: Poems - April 2023

Calling It

Conversing, my offense
Silence, your defense

As I cannot make heads or tails of you
flipped I remain

Carelessly flicked, thumb snaps index

Whoosh

Whoosh

Whoosh

Whoosh

Whoosh

Heads over tails over heads over tails
I don't know which one to call

It makes no difference, either one
I'm undone those first moments I fall

There are times it feels
Life has been one bitter pill
after another

from Cadence: Poems - April 2023

Sleep is My Siren

Sleep is my siren, is my call
to lay my head down, to forget it all
to close weary eyes, to rest my heavy head
to dream of you back in my bed
Strong, smooth arms encircling me
Speaking in hushed voices under cool sheets
That is where I am most at home
But tonight?
Alas, tonight I must lay here alone

It's come to pass, a long held belief
held both close to the vest, and on my sleeve
that not knowing great love is the price I pay for being me

It's not in my nature to run from the light, but rather towards it
towards the care, the arms, the company, the energy of another
Yet my history has shown that I am better off alone

Because the truth of who I am is too harsh
when viewed in the daylight or for any length of time
and I wish to avoid those who don's care to see

This belief is in my blood, in my bones, marrow, veins
It is the electricity that sparks my pulse, my heart, my brain waves

I'm wired *so very differently*

The level of pretending that is required of me
in relationships thus far
is not sustainable

Even when I thought I'd chosen better, smarter
more honestly, more consciously
and when I had been genuinely dedicated, transparent, supportive
it was returned as a consuming fire

Not a blaze of passion or a devouring desire though
No, the fires I experienced were deeply rooted in
resentment and disdain
Those burn differently
Those held me firmly in place at the stake
where their molten bitterness and rage could best engulf me

I burned

I burned for days
and days
and days

I'd still be burning if not for the spirit within me
She is the essence of the phoenix, the Amazon, the fighter
She is the philosopher, the poet, the artist
She rose up within me, and with her came
the strength, power, and courage I possessed all along
Her spirit was the truth of my inner self
reminding me who I am and who I still want to be

Because of her I will no longer burn
except for the fires in my belly
that fuel my way toward a higher plane
A plane where I continue to rise and be reborn
Now, each time I burn
it will be of my own design

But yes, it has come to pass, a long held belief
both close to the vest and on my sleeve
that not knowing great love is the price I pay for being me

Once you've said all you needed to say
make your decision, accept and wait

Whatever you've chosen to do, or not do, it is what it is
no matter how much it may end up helping or or not

Once you've said all you needed to say
make your decision, accept and wait

When the raven comes
with his, "Nevermore"
which, to you, sounds like, "Never again"
know that the black bird's message rings true

You need to let go
You can't hold onto everything
to everyone you've ever loved
Not for forever

Nevermore allow the pain

Nevermore entertain suffering
Nevermore, forever more

Nevermore
Nevermore
Nevermore

Now I Lay Me Down to Sleep

Yes, I believe in ghosts, but what haunts me the most?
More than misty CCTV figures in abandoned warehouses?
More than questionable orbs versus light play?
More than the sound of heavy footsteps when I'm home alone?
More than those, what haunts me most
are the questionable decisions lurking in my past
Those frightening footnotes fold into the shadows
aging me with their bittersweet memories
They were the journeys only I could take
The lessons I'd only learn by living through them
Red flags I would need to ignore to better understand
"Never again" and "Nevermore"

At times my life feels like a cautionary tale

All those poorly made decisions (God help me)
Decisions bearing the names of men
bearing nicknames like
Brooklyn Bad Boy, Highway Guy, the Circus Act, Dull Giant

Many nights these are the ghosts that hold me hostage
depriving me of sleep, their names sprinkled with regret, sadness
stupidity and yes, at times, hilarity
Mostly they serve as undeniable reminders of
my own humanity, fearlessness, and a touch of naivete

Yet even more than all of this, all these misguided moments
what terrifies me most is repeating my history
either in part or in whole

That fear is why I leave the lights on in my head
why the door to my heart is closed off
bolted shut with not one, not two, but three solid locks
why blackout shades are drawn over the windows to my soul
why my, "Hello", is guarded
why I process information like a door cam
noticing everything and recording it for future reference

Yes, I believe in ghosts, but what haunts me the most?
That one final and painful decision, the one bearing his *given* name
the name that undid *every* lock, unarmed *every* alarm
and *drew back* the curtains to let in the light

In the end, it was the light that exposed him
That's what did us in

And so, he is cursed to walk this earth lacking a soul
leaving me to watch for monsters masquerading as lovers
to lock my heart up again...one (click), two (click), three (click)
to draw the shades even tighter than before
to shine brighter lights and secure more vantage points

He is cursed to walk this earth soulless and unfeeling
leaving me alone to say my bedtime prayers

"Now I lay me down to sleep..."

Just out of my reach
again, I might add, again
Go on then, pursue your heart

Self-Preservation

Whomever you choose to love, love them no more than yourself
This way, you have a chance of surviving them
of surviving their departure and the aftermath

I realize this is not a romantic thing to say
yet there is only so much of you
only so much of yourself you can lose
before there is no more of you left to be loved

I've been down on the idea of hope lately
It's been increasingly more elusive for me
So much so that I've felt like a fraud when
trying on the being optimistic part of it
It's been ill suited to me for some time now

Not that I don't *want* to carry that cheeriness inside of me
or to be one who carries light with her everywhere she goes
It's simply been increasingly more foreign to me to believe in it

(Sigh)

I'm not sure I'm explaining myself well

Its been forever now
This painfully long time estranged from optimism
All that glorious sunshine and warmth *just out of my reach*
My spirit is wary, too weary from surviving
the aftermath of so many beat downs

And yet, I admit
there may still be a chance for me to get down with hope again

I'll admit to missing the weightlessness that comes from
holding hope close to me

And as I say this, please know that I don't take you lightly
Not you, not your unwavering love and delight in me
or your limitless support and encouragement
None of it is lost on me
My struggles are rooted in leaden days and nights
They are no reflection on you or the care you have for me

I say all this and ask you not to give up on me
Please keep loving me and being by my side in the way only you can

In return, I promise you
there may still be a chance for me to get down with hope again

Moonbeams

I promise, if I could dance right now, I would

Close to the Vest

No one knows your heart as well as you do
They simply can't know, not your joys or your heartaches
your happiness or your worries, your range of emotions or anxieties
none of it, really, no matter how close they are
or how great the communication with them, to them, is

And that's all okay, though it becomes more isolating at times
You're the only you there is, so when you find people who get you
consider it a blessing and dwell in those connections

But still, even in those safe spaces, only you know yourself so well
so intimately, with profound understanding
It's important that you realize this, and if you don't yet
start cultivating your self-awareness now

Because decisions will need to be made
as to when it would be best to keep yourself to yourself
to keep it all to yourself, to keep it close to the vest

Hope can be tricky
Make you feel things in the dark
the light can't define

from Cadence: Poems - April 2023

Duplicitous Love

Rise above another's duplicitous love
like a bird remembering the freedom of its wings
designed to carry it away from, and also towards

Let the haters plot and draw their swords
Let them twist your words to profit their cause
Unsheathed from lies, the known truth cuts through
Truth is always truth and it will fight for you

Remember that while your enemy presents one way publicly
when they are alone, in the soulless darkness of their dirty rooms
they grind their teeth in private despair

For the one they most cowardly, forcibly rail against
the one they seek to devour and destroy
is the very one they secretly mourns the loss of
as they know in their bones, no one else can compare

Burnt

The thing about being burned is that afterwards
you continue to watch for signs of fire
You know to your core that smoke
is never just smoke
those doorknobs, hot to the touch
aren't doors meant for you
You see the haze, feel the heat rising
the ash dreamily drifting down
catching on your clothes
resting on your eyelids
You taste the destruction in the distance
feel the dry air clinging to you
air with every ounce of life sucked out of it

The thing about getting burned is, afterwards
you forever know that your best line of defense is
to stop, drop and roll the hell away
from the raging, roaring, swelling flames
Even as those flames burn both inside
and outside your scarred self
knowing there will never be enough balm
to soothe your soul deep aches

The Big Picture

If you desire someone else's life, remember this
you cannot pick and choose which parts you experience
Their awards and victories come paired with
burdens and sacrifices
To possess what you desire most about them
you'd also need to own the entirety of their lives
Their every moment, every history, every memory
every twist and turn, fist thrown and ego burn
every overarching ache and bottomless loss

If you desire someone else's life, consider this
Consider the big picture
the *bigger* picture

You may discover than in doing so
you do not want their everything after all

Thrive Now

No matter how long it's been, whether days, months or years
the truths of his lies may still haunt you
The images of his deceit alone are branded into your brain
and the depths of his depravity continue to shred you

You rise above because you have to
because you must keep moving forward
You know this has changed you
will never leave you
will forever be a part of you
But you must not let it define you
or keep you from being your best, most wonderful self

Thrive now
Thrive not because of what or how or why
he did what he did to you
but because of how you've chosen to respond
because you want to excavate a new life
because you want to frame out a new future

Rise up from the shadows of your disappointment
Allow your determination to fortify you
Elevate yourself
Design your days around your dreams
Boldly build on the foundation of your scars

This is me bidding the year good-bye
This is me thanking the last three hundred and sixty-five days
for delivering the painful realness I deserved
and in the way that it did
for knowing it wouldn't have come to me otherwise
for knowing the bracing cold water it threw in my face
was the exact and jarring wake up call I needed
for knowing it had to be a clean break

This is me thanking the course of the planets
for providing additional strength to my bones

This is me thanking the moon and the stars for the proof
that my instincts were in peak form

This is me thanking them all for guiding me with a deep
abiding love, an abundance of unwavering self-respect
and eventually, peace beyond my understanding

This is me bidding the year good-bye while thanking the Cosmos
for the strength to not only withstand the resentment
the contempt felt for me, but also the failings of those who were
and who remain forever, lacking

Give your pain a name
Give a name to the object of your anger
to the reason for your disappointment
to the cause of your discontent

Once you've chosen the name
say that name out loud and at the top of your lungs
This *is not* the time to hold back
Shout out that name while raising your fist in defiance

Show your pain
the object of your anger
the reason for your disappointment
the cause of your discontent
that you are stronger, fiercer, smarter than it is

Resolve to not be silenced, shamed, underestimated
or to otherwise to diminish yourself to appear less than you are
Refuse be squashed or gaslighted
You *will not* be manipulated or beaten down

Show your demons you are the boss of you *and* of them too

I know this may sound strange to some
to call out what is lurking in the shadows
to draw out what thrives in the darkness and expose it to the light
but when you do
when you show your claws and bare your teeth
when you are bold and brave, it's that side of you
the sight of you standing your ground
that will cause the object of your anger
the reason for your disappointment

the cause of your discontent
to tuck tail and run

Give your pain a name
Say that name out loud and at the top of your lungs
This *is not* the time to hold back

First, he made my bed for me
Now he's roasting a chicken for us
Then there are dishes to be done and laundry to be sorted

He simply showed up for me, even as his own cold lingers
even as he worked multiple double shifts over several days
He said he wanted to see me so badly, to have me in his sight
to do what he could for me, to bring me comfort
and so, here he is, asking what needs to be done
asking what he can help me with
and then doing it

Me, with sciatic pain flaring again, leaving me feeling defeated
Me, with a memorial event tomorrow
the one I'd been preparing to lead for months
Me, flat out on the heating pad he set up for me to rest on
as he handles one mundane but necessary task after another

Him being here of his own accord, out of his love for me
out of his need to *show* me the love he has for me
put all of it together and my day has been redeemed

I promise, if I could dance right now, I would
I promise, as soon as I can dance again, I will

Bookends

We are bookends
to each other's days
Beginning
ending
with the other
with stories gathered
with stories shared
in between

Safe Harbor

My head of short grey hair paired with slightly flushed cheeks
rests peacefully on his cool white cotton t-shirt fresh from the dryer
I'm convinced this is the very definition of delight
His chest is wide and a little soft
yet his heartbeat is strong and his love for me is solid

I feel safe here
I *am* safe here
I always am
I always have been

Here is where warm, dark skin meets night chilled alabaster
where my bones quiet down as he cradles me
me and my dreams, for as long as I allow

So why then have my thoughts start to swirl
like the winds of a testy summer storm?
Why is my heart bouncing about like
a rickety craft on restless waters?
It seems an uneasiness has arrived
and it's determined to carry me away, to isolate and shipwreck me
to replace my safe harbor with untold harm

I tell myself to breathe deeply
I steady my nerves, remind myself I can calm the building waves
though they are ruled by an inward, wayward moon
that I can remain in this safe harbor
where his love holds me best, and for as long as I please

And so, I choose to anchor myself
to return to the peace of my safe harbor

I feel safe here
I *am* safe here
I always am
I always have been, and will continue to be
for as long as I allow

I always knew you were on loan
Never all mine, never mattered
Your heart, my home
But still, Society rules Love well

Returning to my bed as my house of cards fell
you've been more than a lover, more than a friend
You're my confidant, a pair of comforting shoulders
supremely kissable lips, arms that shore me up when I am weak
an experienced guide and doting admirer
my fiercest advocate and fellow adventurer
Together we are wholly, wonderfully unconventional

It's been ideal for us both
our love, our devotion
even with everything we know about each other, our circumstances
Our connection has been restorative, genuine, honest
generous, supportive, kind, deep
Together we are a new experience, each for the other

What we are has always remained true for me
There's only you for me
Even on loan with that loan now coming due
There are no regrets for having loved you
No regrets for having been loved *by* you

Footloose

I'd like to think I'll know him
when I see him, speak with him
When the one thing that has hasn't clicked before finally does
Then it'll be hard for me
to remain cynical any longer

Until then I live footloose
dancing
to my own rhythm
twirling
to the music of my heart
howling
at the moon
delighting
in my own existence

When he finds me
he will find me dancing
free, fearless, and footloose

May we find our peace
despite all we are facing

An uphill climb
A downward spiral

We are not alone
even in our darkest moments

Today marks the time
another pass around the sun
another several full phases of the moon
another canopy raised and arching
another cluster of roots spread underground

You're more grounded now than before
You've mended, tended to your broken heart
redirected your thoughts to loftier ones
nourished yourself with good energy and caring people

Today marks the time
It is what it is
Now then, get up love, and move further on

One foot firmly planted, rooted
One foot raised for higher ground
One hand holding for a steady stance
the other stretched up, reaching for my chance

Solidarity

Once again, should you need reminding or to hear it for the first time
it's understood that only a few others, a few, solid, loyal others
will care to know, will seek out so they are *sure* to know
who you are at your core

It may well be that it is only you and them
while the rest of the world doesn't see you, doesn't comprehend you
doesn't get how you process life, how you *live* your life

It is this knowledge, this hope, this solidarity and comradery
with those in your circle, that will fortify you
sustain and steady you, bolster and buoy you
It will raise you above the clamor, the unkindness
the assumptions set in motion to cloud and muddy
the perception of others, others who may
in their ignorance or lack of depth
choose to be deceived about you

Hold fast to those few others, those few, solid, loyal others
who care to know, who seek out so they are *sure* to know
who you are at your core

Embrace the Suck

You're going through something real right now
Real stuff that's knocking you down, making you feel less than
making you feel like you are nobody, to no one
making you feel like you'll be sick forever
tired, lost, depressed *forever*

Maybe you're raising kids on your own
wanting to raise them to be smart, kind, happy
maybe you're doing this while also pursuing
your own education or new career
Maybe it's your third career change
Maybe it's your third marriage
Maybe you're still surviving relationships
the ones you regret having been in
the ones you regret not having moved forward with
or even the ones you, regretfully, revisited
Maybe you've lost loved ones to the grave
Maybe it was due to the consequences of their own actions
or the reckless choices of another's

Life can certainly be a real shit time of it
yet here you are, showing up for it everyday
putting one foot in front of the other
and I'm so happy that you are!

As someone who knows first hand how hard a day
a week, a month, a year, a lifetime can be
I must encourage you to embrace the suck when Life serves it up

Yes indeed, embrace it

Pull that beast right into your chest and squeeeeze!
And yes, at first this will appear to be equal parts madness
and contrary to the "Just be positive" movement
To that I say that to embrace the suck is quite possibly
the most positive of all actions you can take!

Hug the *fuck* out of the suck!
Hold that monster close!
Show it that you're unafraid!
Go ahead and whisper affirmations to it while you're at it!

These actions on your part effectively disarm it
and the moves designed against you
moves to bury you in worry, anxiety
moves meant to rob you of happiness, joy, peace
Embrace the suck and it will no longer have power over you

And yes, you'll still be facing whatever challenge is before you
but you've now shown the suck, and yourself
that you, it's intended victim?
You are in fact a *most capable, most worthy* adversary!

If you doubt my words, then I ask you to indulge me:
Embrace the suck just once and tell me how it didn't change you

Bella Luna

Healing changes you

I walked along here
taking in the warmth and light
like when I'm with you

Evolution

As I took broad steps down a once often trod lane
I found, despite much time, everything remained unchanged
The liars were still lying, the ugliest of hearts were even more so
and those who claimed to have no game were the gamiest of them all

It soon became clear to me as I kept on my way
that while nothing in these others had been improved upon
(they had, in fact, grown darker, more gnarled roots)
the difference was in me, in my resolve to live more consciously

The desire I once nurtured to guide others to be their best
was now nestled in my own heart
set to further *my own* evolution
I always want to be growing
moving towards the best version of myself
To remain static, stagnant, is not something I can do
The need to adapt is strong for me
The pull to learn and adjust comes naturally to me

To remain unchanged, to not be curious about the world
or the lives lived in it, to not want to glean wisdom
from the experiences of others is, to me
one of the saddest of the human conditions

From a Life Well Lived

Simply live your life
Let others live theirs, too
Use common sense
Choose your friends wisely
Read. A lot.
Listen to your gut
Do the things that make you happy and feed your soul
Give to others in need and do it quietly, humbly
Be kind to strangers and animals
Enjoy the simple pleasures of a sandwich and a good cup of coffee
a summer breeze, a sparrow on her nest in the windowsill
Eat chocolate because you can, and because its delicious
Oil vinegar salt and pepper are all the salad dressing you need

And if you should meet someone who appreciates all that you are
if they can keep pace with you, be adventurous and fun with you
and share in your love of deep belly laughs?

Then by all means, enjoy them, too

- inspired by the life of our late Grandma Dolly

Redemption

I hold fast to the belief that when I care, when I give, when I love
when it's done trusting another person
even though they had set out to deceive me
it's my hope that in those moments, at those crossroads
my true intent, my true heart, will be seen, will be understood
and, if needed, will be my redemption releasing me from all my folly

Be grateful for those moments
when you're able to gracefully let go
If that time hasn't come yet, it will
Be ready for it
You'll know when it's arrived

It comes alongside you when, in accepting what is
you go on to live your life accordingly

Bonus! Peace is its companion

The sunrise is late
I'm inclined to stay in bed
Protesting, I go

You are due for some easy love
Like, after all you've dealt with?
Years lost to a lover who didn't love you back?
Tears shed in disappointment and frustration?
Energy spent, fully invested, with little to no returns?

You are due for some real, beautiful, easy, adventurous, freeing love
I'm talking the real deal with someone who speaks your language

You're not settling
Not again
Not now
Not ever

You, my friend, are due for some easy love

Give thanks for all you've learned
Become more comfortable with the idea of hope
with knowledge gleaned from your past
as it will be your strength as you move forward

As more battles await you, you will enter stronger than before
and leave with a fire in your belly regardless of the outcome

Break Free

We often hold the keys that loosen the chains that bind us
If you're unhappy, feeling tethered, if you're captive to something
or someone that isn't right for you, for your soul
you must gather all your courage with both hands
even as those hands are tied, and escape
Free yourself though it leaves you jagged
Vow to continue mending until you're whole again
sound again, safe and sound and heading for the horizon
where the sun meets the sea
where the earth meets the sky
where the moon mingles with the stars

The Comeback

I believed in someone and their professed love for me
I believed despite knowing what I do about Life
It's no surprise then, though it was heartbreaking
when I had to come out swinging

What I know about Life is
how it knocks you down
knocks you down and out, around the block and back again
I had believed in the vows made only to find myself
lacing up my gloves again, bracing for the fight of my life
determined to make my comeback

There is a primal need to tap into that inner drive
to keep getting up over and over and over again
Staying down, out, flat out, not pushing back?
These aren't options for me
I just don't know how to stay down
I do know who blusters, who bellows
and, more and more often who not to get in the ring with

But should I choose to step onto the mat
should I choose to put up my dukes
choose to summon the scrappy side of myself
and draw on my sense of self-preservation
self-worth, self confidence
then I go in knowing my limits, my strengths
knowing where I am most vulnerable
knowing how to bob and weave

I've developed muscle memory and endurance

I have the training of a champion in how to shift my weight
the way and how to lead, the way and how to hold back
Life has been my sparring partner for some time now
I know all too well about the ropes meant to ensnare me
how to wield my power, my strength, my skill until the bell is rung
until the round, the fight, the battle, is called

I remained the favorite in this most recent fight
the one for my dignity and my heart
I retained my title
Celebrated with my fists held high as
sacred sweat ran
triumphant tears were shed
I was bruised but not beaten
hailed the victor even as brave blood flowed
I wore it all as the badge of a warrior

Hope was back on the horizon

And I'll be here to live in that hope
to fight another day
to keep fighting until that elusive, final blow makes contact
But I promise you, even then I'm not going down without a fight

Healing changes you
and it's okay if you get a little tougher, sharper around the edges
You've traded in your soft all over underbelly
for a well-earned suit of armor
Naturally, the trade makes it more difficult
for your enemies to harm you, overpower and pierce you
But that's kind of the point

Some of life's best moments were never planned
They were spontaneous adventures
wrong turns taken in error or on a whim
out of character choices that lead to
unexpected, momentous, even life-enhancing outcomes

On a small scale there are bonfires, cookouts, porch sittings
meteor showers, solar eclipses, shooting stars to wish on
There are movies projected onto sheets suspended in the yard
random joy rides heading lakeside with your best blanket
filling up on gas station hot dogs, root beers and chips
driving until your soul says, "Stop!"

Learn how to cultivate spontaneity in your day
Leave room for the unexpected, for little surprises
Look around, look up, entertain your curiosity
that wonderful notion of not knowing yet, but of wondering

Because some of life's best moments were never planned

A Dark Side

Something bad happened to someone who was bad to me
and in response, I experienced a giddiness that I welcomed

I say this knowing full well some will consider it a character flaw

The realization that I could be happy with another's misfortune
in part because of whose misfortunate it was
prompted me to embrace this dark side of myself

To be fair, there *was* a moment of weighing and measuring
of checking in with my moral compass as I'm known to do
But in the end I chose to accept, even appreciate
the shadow cast on me, me whose creed is to do no harm

I chose to accept this about myself because freedom, to me
means acknowledging *all* of who I am
not just the parts that are pretty
(and let's face it, the prettier parts are easier to love)

I grew up understanding that my feelings came dead last
after everyone else's, even those who hurt me
disrespected me, had disdain for me
Validation and a sense of self weren't really fostered in my home
Later in life, I would consciously set out to retrain my head and heart
Debugging my motherboard looked a lot like therapy
setting boundaries, drawing myself out after years of being invisible

Being loyal to myself comes easier now, but I've always fought for
those closest to me, those in my circle, my tribe
Standing up for myself always felt instinctive, but it was squashed

labeled too bold, too individual, too selfish
Therefore it became something I needed to cultivate over time

And yes, sometimes my passion is misunderstood
though most of the time it's appreciated and admired
I know my heart, my thought processes, my baseline
I accept and mourn the misconceptions about me
They come from me being fierce, protective, and emboldened

There are some who fear the dark side
they're uncomfortable with *their* dark side
with what they think it says about them to have one
so much so that they dissuade others from acknowledging their own

For me though, I choose to embrace my darkness
especially because, more often than not,
I still choose to first embrace my light

Have you forgotten the value of floating?
Of calming yourself when the seas grow wild?

from Cadence: Poems - April 2023

Always, always, always shut out the noise
the nonsense, the naysayers, the detractors
Shut them all out
Be true to yourself
Do what you need to do, what you must do, for yourself

You needn't listen to everyone's opinions
misconceptions of you, of your situations
If you did, there would be no liking yourself, no respecting yourself
no self-confidence, no self-preservation, no happiness

Your goal is to not just like yourself,
but to *love* yourself, to *respect* yourself
to show yourself, and others, what you stand for
when it comes to you and your unique existence

Looking at all you've done and the heart you've done it with
the spirit it's been done in with the certainty you've known all along
Looking at it all I say
there is no greater ally for you than your truest self

Be a Thorn

Be a difficult woman and raise your voice
Fight for your freedoms, for liberty and justice for all
Make uncomfortable the seat of the unjust
Rock the foundation of their foothold

Shake it up!
Shake *them* up
Wake them from their slumber, challenge them
at every angle, every toehold, every hill, every mountain

Don't for one second let them believe you are content in the valley

Be the thorn they don't fear as they fuss over your bloom
over your rosy appearance, looking enticing while on display
though you were quite content to stay rooted and growing freely
Plucked for their own pleasure, they view you only as
something to be contained and controlled

They know that to separate you from yourself means you will wither
They know that to remove you from yourself means you will die

Their attention span is fleeting, subjective, utterly toxic

Make noise!
We clamor to know a fraction of the life they've been birthed into
We raise our voices, shield our bodies, fight for our basic rights
as they take their well-honed knives to our throats
to our bellies, to our souls

They think nothing of their duality, their cruelty, their hatred

their patriarchy, masked behind the founding fathers
Fathers who ruled, yes, but while they ruled
the founding mothers dissented

You ask me, "How do I know they dissented?"
I ask you, "Where do you think your fire came from?"

It grew from heritage seeds sown and reaped
by thousands upon thousands of women from every generation
reaching back to the original garden, regenerating for centuries

They too were thorns with passions and voices
with ideas, convictions, beliefs and dreams
while also presenting the rosiest of dispositions

And so I say again, be a thorn

When You're Ready

When will you lift your face to the sun?
Open your arms to the sky?
Lift open hands to the moon?
Peer in wonder again at the stars?
Stand tall on the sand?

Take your time, but also know that when you're ready
The wind waits to enfold you, to hold you, to dry your tears

When you're ready, the Universe will carry your grief
as a sacred offering of their memory, in their honor

When you're ready, bring all that's been broken
everything shattered, shards and dust alike

When you're ready, gather it all up, carry them close to you
heal as you go while still sharing in all that is ahead

When you're ready
lift your face to the sun
open your arms to the sky
lift open hands to the moon
peer in wonder again at the stars
and, once again, stand tall on the sand

Go out, and be daring
Be brilliant, amazing, unstoppable, influential

Get our of your own way, out of your comfort zone
Be wise and safe, but not so safe that you stunt your growth

Be bold and adventurous
Make memories to carry with you into old age

Above all, be open
Open your beautiful soul to receive all that the Universe has for you

You have one life and it's the only life that can be lived by only you
Go live it and live it big

The Brush

Oh, to be the brush that paints the portrait of his heart
To be the very instrument by which he makes his mark
With each directing stroke to canvas
eye to I relate a vision only he can see
until led in the dance, with me

- for Steve

Together

The weight of the world's ills fall
not on one person's shoulders, but on us all
To carry it best, we must walk in step, together
We must gauge the path, the pitfalls, the roadblocks, together
Together, in unison, step by step, hand in hand
We are stronger, *so much stronger*, together, as one

Promise me
you'll continue to be kind to yourself, to feed your soul
to choose more wisely in all areas of your life
to keep loving yourself for all your unique qualities

Promise me
you'll find ways to do that if you've forgotten how

Promise me you'll accept yourself
all your earned scars and radiant points of light

Promise me that above all, you will respect yourself
Promise me that you'll live to be free

Stardust

It's okay if your ship has sailed
It could have been another Titanic

Don't say,

"I could never do that to someone I love",

because, trust me, you could

———————

It may take all kinds, but there are some kinds I can't take

———————

LOVE IS OPAQUE. RESPECT IS CLEAR.

———————

The time is coming when the devil you know won't be worth knowing

Peace of mind is fairly priceless,
though it may cost you a great deal
more to obtain it

———❦———

Ever feel like you closed your eyes to make a wish on a candle

only to find that someone stole your cake?

———❦———

Don't be the person who feels obliged to fill the silences

———❦———

MAYBE DÉJÀ VU IS SIMPLY YOU

COMING BACK AROUND AGAIN

Resigning yourself to your fate may go against every fiber of your being, but on the other hand, fighting for more, for better, is exhausting and, at times, it can feel so futile

---

SOME FOLKS ARE PROS AT BEING CONS

You have to ask the hard questions

even though you already know the answers

MAYBE YOU NEED TO THROW THE ROPE OUT

AND SAVE YOURSELF

It can be difficult to grasp that things didn't go the way you thought they would. Then there are times when things not going the way you thought they would actually turn out better than you ever imagined possible.

The thing about wisdom, signs, and experiences is they only teach you if you're willing to learn from them. If you don't, they'll just wait around for someone else who is.

If today marks something for you, take a deep breath. Exhale and know that it is what it is. Know that you will be okay. Now then, get up and move on.

If they busted up your world in the past, they are not welcome in your present while you're building your future. Come to think of it, they're not welcome in your future either.

Always listen to your gut.
It's usually right when telling you something is wrong

———✦———

You'll find in life everyone disappoints you, even,
and possibly most often, you'll disappoint yourself

———✦———

Know your strengths and play them
Know your weaknesses to not get
played

———✦———

BEING YOUR BEST SELF OFTEN MEANS

LEARNING TO LOVE WHAT'S GOOD FOR YOU

Staying positive can only get you so far
Then there will be times you'll need it to get you farther

———◈———

LEARN TO BE COMFORTABLE WITH
TAKING A FEW STEPS BACK.
YOU MAY DISCOVER THAT IN DOING SO
YOU ACTUALLY COME OUT AHEAD.

———◈———

One kind word from an otherwise unkind person doesn't suddenly make them kinder. More likely, they just experienced a momentary lapse of character.

———◈———

You were built to fly. Don't let anyone clip your wings.

Someone always knows the truth
Be sure that someone is you

AT TIMES, IT WILL BE DIFFICULT BEING

THE PERSON YOU PROFESS YOU WANT TO BE

SLEEP, LIKE A LOVER WHOSE COMPANY YOU CHERISH,
MAY STILL LEAVE YOU WANTING

Knowledge is power

The key though, is *what knowledge?*

and then, *what power?*

Only what is known can set you free

Knowledge is of no use while it remains hidden

Epilogue

And so, the story continues
the proverbial chapters change
one ending, another beginning
There is no jumping ahead
no skipping to the end

No, you must follow in the order written
Miss none of the meanings
Engage in all the plot twists
Follow each character development
Absorb all the author intends

The author, you
Though it is by trial and error
your full tale will continue to unfold

Early Spring Moon, Terryville, CT
Author

Acknowledgements

Natalie Jury, Brenda Crowell, RT Jury, Emily Jury, Earl Punter, Scott & Carmen Schaffer, Shylock Therrien, and Jenn Mowry ... *You continue to be a source of love and support for me, and that has made all the difference! Thank you!*

Dr. Megan Schmidt, Dr. Jo'an Tankou, St. Francis Hospital, Hartford, CT, and the Visiting Nurse & Hospice of Litchfield County staff ... *It's because of your medical skill and care that my outlook on the future is bright! Thank you!*

Cadence and I partnered with the following groups in 2023 to promote my debut publication. Their support of the arts is a necessity, with many writers and artisans having benefitted from it. ... *Thank you for supporting this writer in the pursuit of her passion!*

Artistic Outlets
The CT Poetry Guild
The Bristol Bazaar

Community Events
White Memorial Family Nature Day
Main Street Torrington Christmas Holiday Fair

Libraries & Bookshops
The Bristol Public Library
The Avon Free Public Library
The Curious Cat Bookshop

Media Coverage
The Bristol Press
The Author on Wheels Podcast
WAPJ 89.9 FM & 105.1 Community Radio

The following fellow Indie Authors & Artists are both friends and peers who have cheered me on and inspired me with their own artistic journeys. They represent a wide variety of genres, from non-fiction and poetry to fantasy and adventures, and they're based around the world! *Please visit their socials listed below to learn more!*

Stacey Dexter
staceydexterwriter.com/

Cameron Trost
linktr.ee/camerontrost

J.D. Brubaker
linktr.ee/j.d.brubaker

J.L. Henry
Jameslouishenry.com

Wendy Haller
linktr.ee/wendyhals

Joe Adomavicia
www.facebook/joeadomavicia

Tara Baja
www.facebook/TaraBajaAuthor

Tessy Braun
www.facebook.com/Tessy.braun.writer

Rich Cyr
www.facebook.com/richtheclawcyr/

Special thanks to **Rich Cyr** for having me as a guest on The Claw's Corner video podcast early in 2024! The interview will have aired on May 12, 2024, the Sunday leading up to the release of *Behind the Blue*. Check it out at The Claw's Corner on YouTube and other major podcast streaming platforms!

Author Bio

Like so many fellow wordsmiths she's met along the way, Sharon Arsego's journey into creative writing began in elementary school. As a child, both her library and her portable, putty colored manual typewriter were all gleaned from local yard sales.

That typewriter was a treasure and a tangible taste of what Arsego envisioned a writer's life would be like. Her growing appreciation for words and creative writing were soon set to, and nurtured by, that machine's soothing tap-tap rhythm.

While the little conduit of dreams has long been lost to time and household moves, Arsego never forgot the role it played in helping her find her passion. Though it would be many moons later, with quiet computers replacing chatty typewriters, the publication of *Cadence* in 2023 was her childhood dream realized. With more works to come, Arsego feels she would be remiss if she didn't acknowledge her first little typewriter and the love it showed her all those years ago.

Born and raised in Connecticut, Arsego currently lives and works in Bristol. When not writing or reading, she enjoys binge-watching on various streaming platforms, sharing adventures with family and friends, and supporting local libraries as well as independent authors and artists in the global community. She also shares a love for cheese with her feline rescue, Mack.

Additional Works by the Author
Cadence: Poems

Facebook: SwirlInkPublications
Author Hub: linktr.ee/sharonarsego

Anthologies & Freelance:
SwirlInkPublications.com

BEHIND THE BLUE: POETRY & PROSE

A SWIRL INK PUBLICATIONS
POETRY COLLECTION